DATE DUE		

Creative Education

MAMMALS

PART TWO

On The Cover:
A Wooly Mammoth.
To protect themselves from
predators, some plant-eating
mammals stayed small—and
some grew very big.
Cover Art by Walter Stuart.

Published by Creative Education, Inc., 123 South Broad Street, Mankato, Minnesota 56001

Printed by permission of Wildlife Education, Ltd.

ISBN 0-88682-396-X

Created and written by
John Bonnett Wexo

Chief Artist
Walter Stuart

Senior Art Consultant
Mark Hallett

Design Consultant
Eldon Paul Slick

Production Art Director
Maurene Mongan

Production Artists
Bob Meyer
Fiona King
Hildago Ruiz

Photo Staff
Renee C. Burch
Katharine Boskoff

Publisher
Kenneth Kitson

Associate Publisher
Ray W. Ehlers

MAMMALS

PART TWO

This Volume is Dedicated to: Bernard Thorton and His Artists. Without them, a project of this size and artistic scope would have been unthinkable. Their combined talents are a national treasure of Great Britain.

Art Credits

Pages Six and Seven: Richard Orr; **Pages Eight and Nine:** Richard Orr; **Page Eight: Top,** Walter Stuart; **Page Nine: Lower Right,** Robert Bampton; **Pages Ten and Eleven:** Richard Orr; **Page Ten: Lower Left,** Robert Bampton; **Page Eleven: Lower Middle, Middle Right and Lower Right,** Robert Bampton; **Pages Twelve and Thirteen:** Richard Orr; **Page Twelve: Lower Left and Middle Right,** Robert Bampton; **Page Thirteen: Upper Left and Right:** Robert Bampton; **Page Fourteen and Fifteen:** Richard Orr; **Page Fifteen:** Horse Hooves, Robert Bampton; **Pages Sixteen and Seventeen:** Richard Orr; **Page Seventeen: Top,** Walter Stuart; **Pages Eighteen and Nineteen:** Richard Orr; **Page Eighteen: Left,** Walter Stuart; **Page Eighteen: Center and Bottom,** Robert Bampton; **Page Eighteen: Center Right,** Walter Stuart; **Pages Twenty and Twenty-one:** Richard Orr; **Page Twenty: Top,** Walter Stuart; **Page Twenty-one: Top,** Walter Stuart; **Page Twenty-one: Lower Left,** Robert Bampton; **Pages Twenty-two and Twenty-three: Background,** Timothy Hayward; **Figures,** Chuck Byron.

Photographic Credits

Page Ten: Tom McHugh *(Photo Researchers)*; **Page Eleven:** Lloyd Beesley *(Animals Animals)*; **Page Thirteen:** John Cancalosi *(Bruce Coleman, Ltd.)*; **Page Seventeen:** Bruce Coleman, Inc.; **Page Twenty-one:** Peter B. Kaplan *(Photo Researchers)*.

Creative Education would like to thank Wildlife Education, Ltd., for granting them the right to print and distribute this hardbound edition.

Contents

Plant-eating mammals took the place of plant-eating dinosaurs. The dinosaurs left **many niches** empty when they died out— and the mammals evolved **many new species** rather quickly to fill the niches. When a group of animals spreads out like this to fill niches, scientists say that the group is **radiating** (RAY-dee-ATE-ing).

As they were radiating, the plant-eating mammals developed new types of **bodies and teeth**—to help them find food and survive in their new niches. Some of them "invented" long trunks that could reach up into trees like the long necks of dinosaurs. Some evolved sharp incisors for cutting nuts and other hard foods. Others developed heavy cheek teeth for grinding up tough plants.

To protect themselves from predators, the plant-eaters changed in many ways. Some evolved **long legs,** so they could run away from predators. Some developed **horns and tusks** and big claws that they could use as weapons. And others had **heavy armor** on the outside of their bodies.

MONKEYS, APES

PRIMATES
(PRY-mates)

Forest dwellers that usually live in trees.

BEAVERS

PORCUPINES

RODENTS
(ROW-dents)

Small animals with incisors that are sharp like chisels.

GROUND SLOTHS

GLYPTODONTS

EDENTATES
(EE-den-tates)

Armored mammals of many sizes.

During the Age of Dinosaurs, mammals were **small creatures.** After the dinosaurs died, these tiny animals evolved into many different animals of many shapes and sizes. Some were small and some were **giants!**

ARTIODACTYLS
(art-ee-uh-DAK-tills)

Animals with **an even number** of toes—usually two or four on a foot.

BISON

LEMURS

DEER AND ANTELOPE

HORSES

Animals with **an odd number of toes** on each foot—usually one or three.

PERISSODACTYLS
(PURR-iss-uh-DAK-tills)

RHINOS

PROBOSCIDEANS
(pro-bah-SID-ee-uns)

Usually large animals with trunks and tusks.

SIRENIANS
(sigh-REE-knee-uns)

Water mammals that eat seaweed and other plants.

SEA COWS

ELEPHANTS

S ome plant-eaters grew very large, and their size was a great advantage for them. You remember that large size helped **to protect** some plant-eating dinosaurs from predators—and it provides similar protection for large mammals. At the same time, large size also made it possible for big mammals **to get food** that was beyond the reach of other animals.

This was lucky, because large animals **need a lot more food** to keep them going. As some mammals got bigger, they were forced to evolve better and better ways of getting food. This is easy to see in the evolution of the **proboscideans** (pro-bah-SID-ee-uns), or elephants.

As elephants got larger and larger, they developed **trunks** to help them reach more food. And **tusks** are also useful in getting food.

LONG TRUNKS

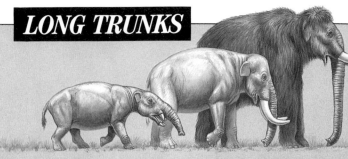

As elephants grew taller, they needed to evolve **longer trunks**. Since they used their trunks to get water, the trunks had to reach down far enough to suck up the water. So—the longer the legs, the longer the trunk!

TEETH INTO TUSKS

The ancestor of all elephants was not very large, and it looked more like a hippo than an elephant. But it did have some **long incisor teeth** Ⓐ—and a rather long **upper lip**.

Over millions of years, the long incisors got much longer—and they evolved into **tusks** Ⓑ. The upper lip got bigger, too. It evolved into **a trunk**!

The pointed tusks of elephants are sometimes used as weapons **to defend them** against predators. But they are used more often **to get food.** During the evolution of the elephants, different types of elephants have used their tusks in different ways to get food.

Some elephants used their tusks **to dig** food out of the ground Ⓒ. Some used them **to dredge up** plants from the water Ⓓ. And others **stripped bark** off trees Ⓔ.

HUGE TEETH

To stay alive, elephants needed big teeth that could chew **a lot of food** every day. And the teeth evolved in a very interesting way. Over millions of years, many small teeth **joined together** Ⓕ to form a few BIG teeth.

Some elephants were leaf-eaters. They evolved teeth with **many small bumps** on them Ⓖ. Each of the bumps worked like a hammer **to crush leaves.**

Other elephants ate grass, and they needed teeth that could **grind the grass.** They evolved teeth made of huge bony plates Ⓗ. To grind, the teeth **moved back and forth** Ⓘ.

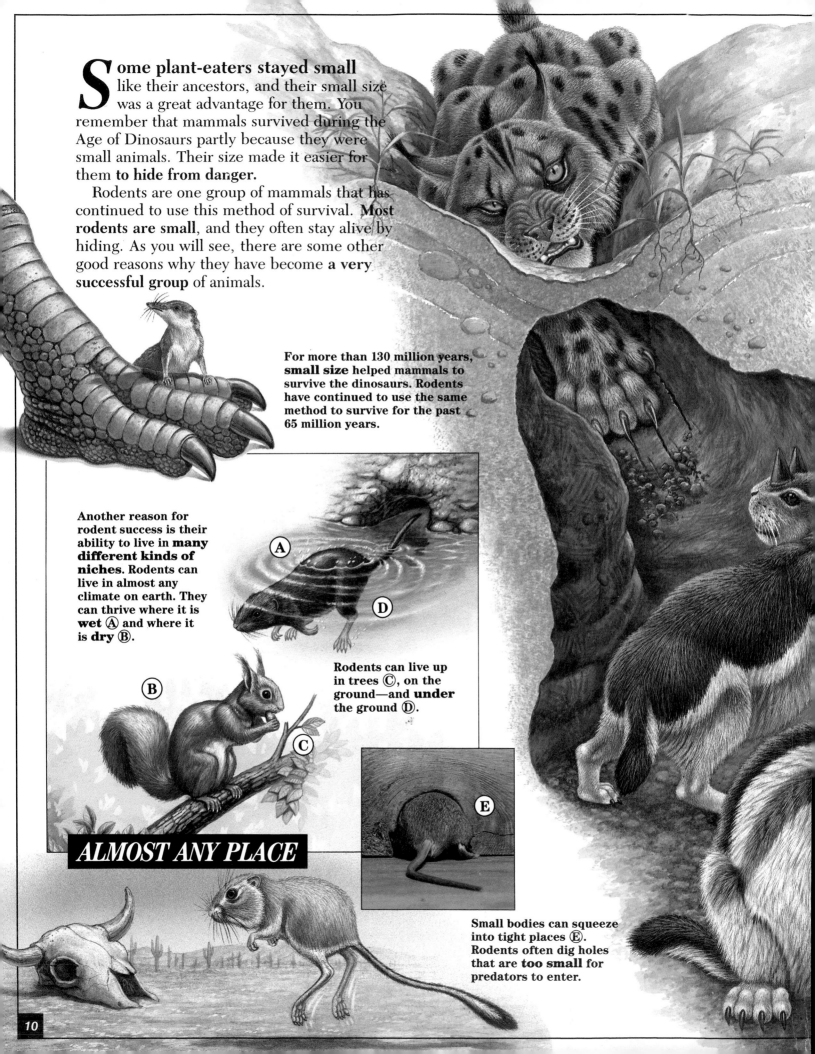

Some plant-eaters stayed small like their ancestors, and their small size was a great advantage for them. You remember that mammals survived during the Age of Dinosaurs partly because they were small animals. Their size made it easier for them **to hide from danger.**

Rodents are one group of mammals that has continued to use this method of survival. **Most rodents are small**, and they often stay alive by hiding. As you will see, there are some other good reasons why they have become **a very successful group** of animals.

For more than 130 million years, **small size** helped mammals to survive the dinosaurs. Rodents have continued to use the same method to survive for the past 65 million years.

Another reason for rodent success is their ability to live in **many different kinds of niches**. Rodents can live in almost any climate on earth. They can thrive where it is **wet** Ⓐ and where it is **dry** Ⓑ.

Rodents can live up in trees Ⓒ, on the ground—and **under the ground** Ⓓ.

ALMOST ANY PLACE

Small bodies can squeeze into tight places Ⓔ. Rodents often dig holes that are **too small** for predators to enter.

If you measure success by **sheer numbers**, rodents are the most successful mammals on earth. There are more of them than all other mammals **put together!** Nearly *half* of all mammal species are rodents.

Rodents also survive because of their incredible ability **to reproduce**. When some rodents are killed, lots of new ones are easily produced to replace them.

ALMOST ANY FOOD

Rodents can also eat almost *anything*. This is partly because they have wonderful teeth—including incisors that are like **sharp chisels** Ⓕ.

The incisors can cut into very hard food, such as nuts—**or even wood**. And the cheek teeth Ⓖ can grind and crush almost anything.

Rodents are also **not very fussy** about *what* they eat. When their normal foods are scarce, they will switch to something else—and survive.

*A*rmored mammals were armored for the same reason that some dinosuars had armor—to give them protection from predators. There were two main types, and each type had a different kind of armor. The **glyptodonts** (GLIP-tuh-dahntz) were covered with bony plates, from the tips of their noses to the ends of their tails. The **ground sloths** (SLAW-th-s) had their armor hidden under a thick coat of shaggy hair.

Like armored dinosaurs, armored mammals were probably peaceful creatures if they were left alone. But if they were attacked, they had **sharp claws** to defend themselves—and many of them had **large clubs** on their tails.

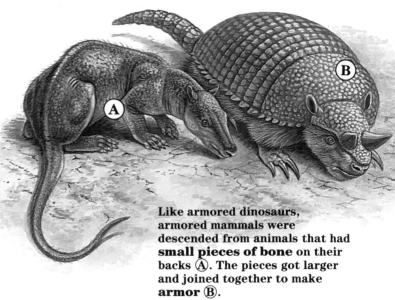

Like armored dinosaurs, armored mammals were descended from animals that had **small pieces of bone** on their backs Ⓐ. The pieces got larger and joined together to make **armor** Ⓑ.

GLYPTODONT ARMOR

GROUND SLOTH ARMOR

Ground sloths had many pieces of bone **inside the skin** Ⓒ. Glyptodonts had many plates of bone **on top of the skin** Ⓓ.

Ground sloths were the largest armored mammals. Some of them were as large as elephants! They liked to sit up and eat leaves from tall trees. They could grab leaves with their **long tongues**—just like giraffes do today.

Like all large animals, ground sloths needed **really big bones** to hold up their big bodies. A few of their bones weighed **50 pounds each.**

HUMAN LEG BONE

GROUND SLOTH LEG BONE

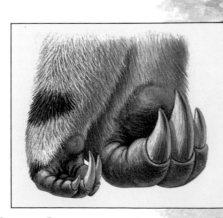

Large claws were used as weapons and for digging up food. Many glytodonts also had **huge clubs** on their tails for defense.

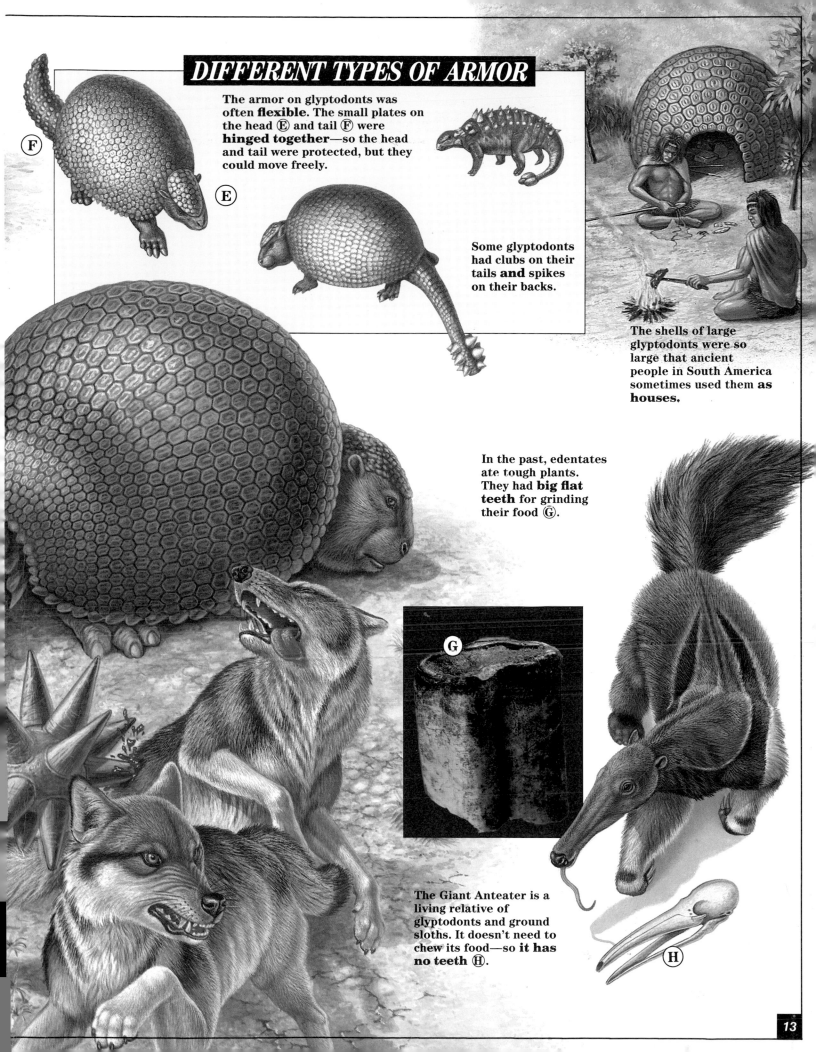

DIFFERENT TYPES OF ARMOR

The armor on glyptodonts was often **flexible**. The small plates on the head Ⓔ and tail Ⓕ were **hinged together**—so the head and tail were protected, but they could move freely.

Ⓕ

Ⓔ

Some glyptodonts had clubs on their tails **and** spikes on their backs.

The shells of large glyptodonts were so large that ancient people in South America sometimes used them **as houses.**

In the past, edentates ate tough plants. They had **big flat teeth** for grinding their food Ⓖ.

Ⓖ

The Giant Anteater is a living relative of glyptodonts and ground sloths. It doesn't need to chew its food—so **it has no teeth** Ⓗ.

Ⓗ

Hoofed **plant-eaters** are generally called **ungulates** (UN-gyou-lits), and many mammals have belonged to this group. They evolved hoofs to help them run away from predators. And most of them developed **longer legs** for the same purpose. For further protection, many of them grew large—and some of them got **really big**.

Today, ungulates are a very successful group of animals. In fact, **all** of the larger plant-eating mammals living today on earth are ungulates.

Hoofs probably evolved from the claws of primitive mammals. They protect and cushion the feet of ungulates, so they can run on hard ground.

The biggest land mammal that ever lived was an ungulate. It was **18 feet high** at the shoulder!

All ungulates today have hoofs. In the past, some still had claws like primitive mammals. The claws were probably used for digging up roots to eat.

Some ungulates developed special body parts for grabbing food— like the **flexible noses** of tapirs.

EVOLUTION OF HORSES

PLIOHIPPUS

4

EQUUS

5

Horses today are much larger than their ancestors, with much longer legs.

6

Hoofed mammals living today are divided into two groups. And you can tell one group from another by counting **the number of toes** on their feet! Horses and rhinos and tapirs belong to a group called **the perissodactyls** (PURR-iss-uh-DAK-tills). They have **an odd number** of toes on their feet—usually one or three toes. As you know, horses today have one large toe on each foot—and this helps them to run very fast. But the first horses had **three toes** on their front feet and four on the back!

MERYCHIPPUS

3

MESOHIPPUS

2

HYRACOTHERIUM

1

Compare the toes of early horses (below) with the toe of a modern wild horse (above). It's easy to see how **evolution has changed horses** over millions of years.

The horns of ancient ungulates took many forms. Some had huge battering rams Ⓑ. And others had **clusters of horns** Ⓒ.

Ⓒ

Ⓑ

In the past, many ungulates looked like tanks, with **horns on their noses** that they used for fighting. Rhinos are the only ungulates of this type living today.

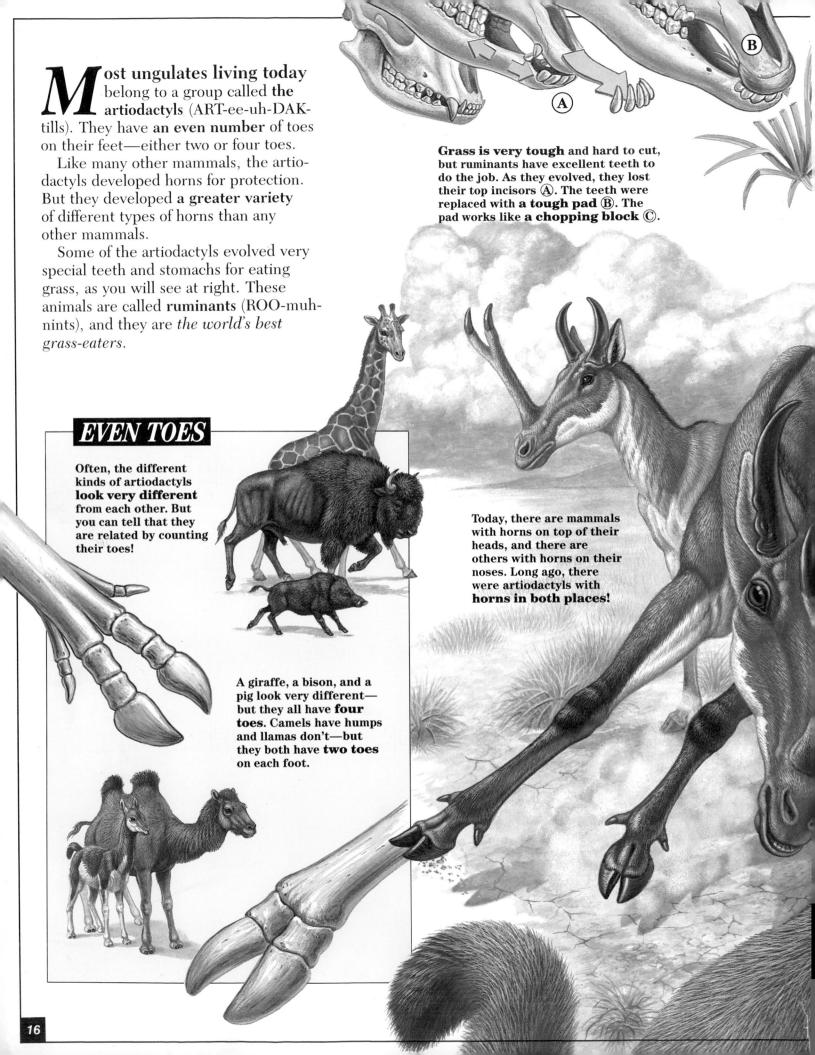

ost ungulates living today belong to a group called **the artiodactyls** (ART-ee-uh-DAK-tills). They have **an even number** of toes on their feet—either two or four toes.

Like many other mammals, the artiodactyls developed horns for protection. But they developed **a greater variety** of different types of horns than any other mammals.

Some of the artiodactyls evolved very special teeth and stomachs for eating grass, as you will see at right. These animals are called **ruminants** (ROO-muh-nints), and they are *the world's best grass-eaters.*

Grass is very tough and hard to cut, but ruminants have excellent teeth to do the job. As they evolved, they lost their top incisors Ⓐ. The teeth were replaced with **a tough pad** Ⓑ. The pad works like **a chopping block** Ⓒ.

EVEN TOES

Often, the different kinds of artiodactyls **look very different** from each other. But you can tell that they are related by counting their toes!

Today, there are mammals with horns on top of their heads, and there are others with horns on their noses. Long ago, there were artiodactyls with **horns in both places!**

A giraffe, a bison, and a pig look very different—but they all have **four toes.** Camels have humps and llamas don't—but they both have **two toes** on each foot.

CHEWING TWICE

1 The grass is neatly chopped off.

2 Grass is so hard to digest that ruminants have to **chew it twice**. The cheek teeth crush it once Ⓓ, and then **it is swallowed** Ⓕ.

4 It goes to the first two stomachs Ⓔ, where **chemicals break down** the tough fibers. Then it goes back to the mouth Ⓕ **for more chewing!**

5 It is swallowed **one more time**, and goes to the third and fourth stomachs Ⓖ. It finally **releases its energy** to the body Ⓗ.

HORNS AND ANTLERS

Horns and antlers are used to fight off predators. They are also used by males to **fight over females** during the mating season.

Some artiodactyls grow new **antlers** every year. Others have permanent **horns**.

The importance of niches in guiding the evolution of animals is easy to see in the way that plant-eating mammals evolved **in South America**. For more than 65 million years, South America was **cut off** from the other continents of the world, like Australia is today. During that long period of time, the animals of South America were **out of touch** with the rest of the animals of the world—they were left to evolve **on their own**.

You might think that they would evolve in very different ways from the animals in the rest of the world. But a remarkable thing happened. Many South American mammals evolved to look **very much like** animals in other parts of the world. This happened because they lived in **similar kinds of niches**.

ANCIENT ELEPHANT

A WORLD APART

Scientists tell us that the continents we live on are **moving**. And they have been moving for many millions of years. They move very slowly, so you can't **see** it happening. But over a long time, continents can travel great distances. About 70 million years ago, South America **moved away from North America**.

For millions of years, there was **a wide area of water** Ⓐ between South America and North America. This water kept most plants and animals from crossing into South America. So the animals of South America were **left alone** to evolve on their own.

There were niches in South America that were similar to the niches of elephants in other parts of the world. The South American mammals that lived in these niches evolved to look **very much like elephants**.

South American animals that lived by rivers like hippos started to **look like hippos**. They had large stomachs in bulky bodies—and short, stubby legs to hold up their great weight.

The tusks on both animals evolved from **upper incisors**.

Both animals had heavy feet. The toes of both could **spread out** to keep both animals from sinking into the mud.

On the plains of South America, there were niches for animals with longs legs that could run fast. So animals evolved that looked very much **like horses**.

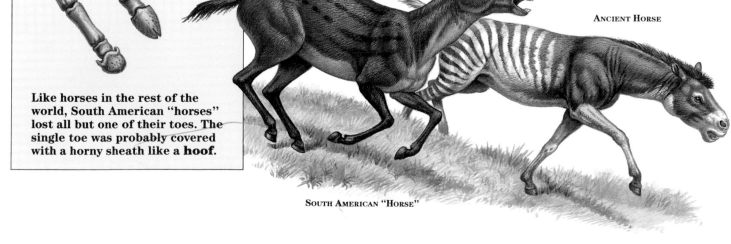

ANCIENT HORSE

Like horses in the rest of the world, South American "horses" lost all but one of their toes. The single toe was probably covered with a horny sheath like a **hoof**.

SOUTH AMERICAN "HORSE"

U p in the trees was a good place to find plenty of **food**, and a good place to **stay safe** from many predators—so some mammals took to the trees. The first mammals to do this were probably insect-eaters during the Age of Dinosaurs. From these little animals, a wonderful group of tree-living mammals called **the primates** (PRY-mates) evolved.

Primates developed special bodies for living in the trees. To keep from falling, they evolved **special hands and feet** that could grab branches and hold on firmly. To judge distances, so they could jump from branch to branch, they evolved **large eyes** that could see three dimensions. To control their complex hands and eyes, the primates developed **more complex brains**—they became more intelligent.

EXCELLENT EYES

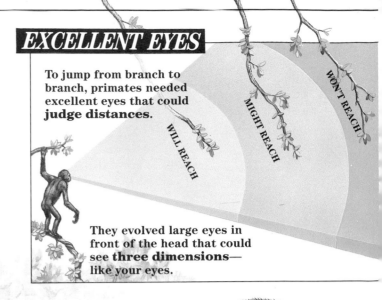

To jump from branch to branch, primates needed excellent eyes that could **judge distances**.

WILL REACH

MIGHT REACH

WON'T REACH

They evolved large eyes in front of the head that could see **three dimensions**—like your eyes.

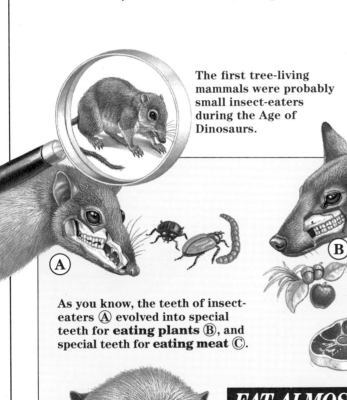

The first tree-living mammals were probably small insect-eaters during the Age of Dinosaurs.

As you know, the teeth of insect-eaters Ⓐ evolved into special teeth for **eating plants** Ⓑ, and special teeth for **eating meat** Ⓒ.

Ⓐ

Ⓑ

Ⓒ

EAT ALMOST ANYTHING

The teeth of most primates did not become too specialized—so they could eat **many different kinds of foods** Ⓓ. You remember that the ability to eat many things helped rodents to survive—and it helped the primates in the same way. Animals that can eat both plants and meat are called **omnivores** (OM-nuh-vorz).

Ⓓ

To climb, primates developed special hands and feet, with long fingers and **the first thumbs**. Most of them could hold on equally well with their hands and their feet.

THUMBS

Thumbs made it possible for primates to grab things better than any other mammal Ⓔ. They could hold on **hard** Ⓕ, or they could hold **gently** Ⓖ. The gentle grip was great for gathering food.

INTELLIGENCE

To look and swing and grab things in trees, primates needed **bigger brains.** They evolved brains that were very large for the size of their bodies. They are probably **the most intelligent mammals** on earth.

For more than 65 million years, most primates have been small animals living in trees. But some have grown larger, and started to spend part of the time on the ground.

REMEMBER:

1 With the dinosaurs gone, the tiny mammals were free to move into many empty niches. **They radiated** and evolved into a wonderful array of different animals.

2 **The variety** of plant-eating animals that evolved was astonishing. Over millions of years, plant-eaters of many shapes and sizes developed.

3 Some plant-eaters grew **very large,** like the elephants. Their size protected them from predators, and they developed tusks and trunks to help them get food.

4 Other plant-eaters **stayed small,** like the rodents—because this was also a good way to stay safe from many predators. Rodents could hide in small places that other animals could not reach.

5 Rodents had teeth that **could eat almost anything.** This helped them to survive when food was scarce.

6 Some plant-eaters developed **armor.** Like armored dinosaurs, they sometimes had **clubs on their tails** to help defend them from predators.

7 Some armored mammals were huge. Ground sloths were covered with shaggy hair, and didn't look like armored animals—but there were small armor plates **in their skin.**

8 **Hoofed mammals** are called ungulates. They often grew to large size, and many of them had large horns on their heads for protection.

9 Today, there are two different kinds of ungulates, and you can tell them apart by **counting their toes!** **Perissodactyls** are ungulates with **an odd number** of toes—usually one or three.

10 **Artiodactyls** are ungulates with **an even number** of toes. Members of this group are famous for their great variety of **horns and antlers.**

NEW WORDS:

Radiating
(RAY-dee-ATE-ing):
Many new animals evolving rather quickly **to fill empty niches.** Mammals were radiating when they filled many niches left empty by dinosaurs.

Proboscideans
(pro-bah-SID-ee-uns):
Elephants and their relatives.

Ungulates
(UN-gyou-lits):
Plant-eating mammals **with hoofs.** All large plant-eating mammals living on earth today are ungulates, except elephants.

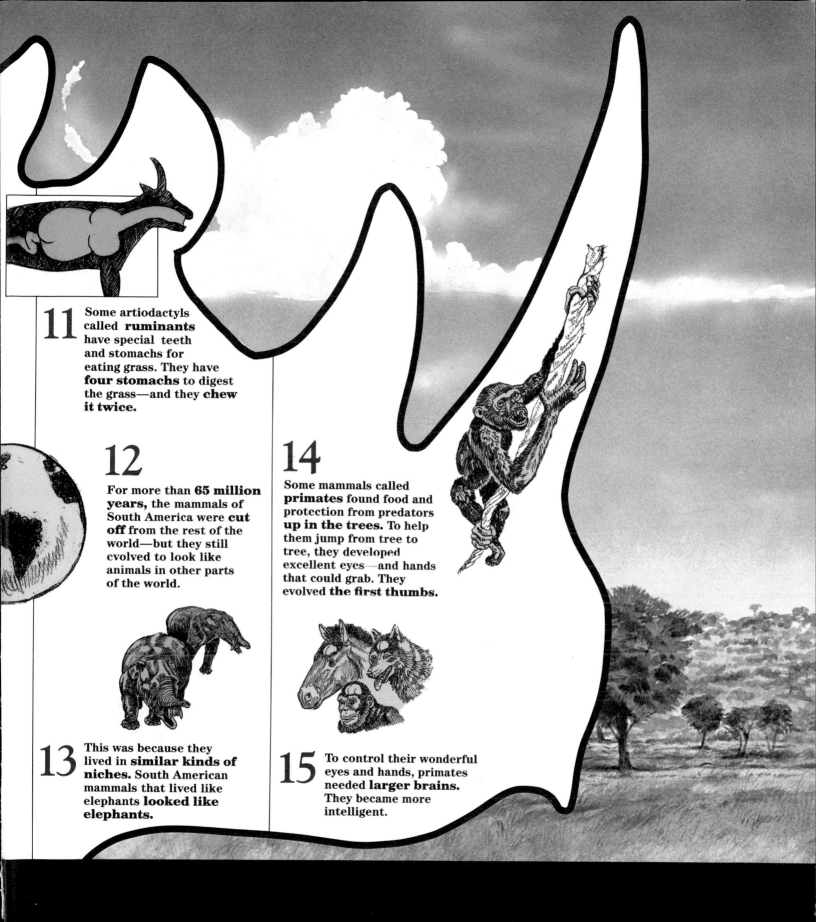

11 Some artiodactyls called **ruminants** have special teeth and stomachs for eating grass. They have **four stomachs** to digest the grass—and they **chew it twice.**

12 For more than **65 million years,** the mammals of South America were **cut off** from the rest of the world—but they still evolved to look like animals in other parts of the world.

13 This was because they lived in **similar kinds of niches.** South American mammals that lived like elephants **looked like elephants.**

14 Some mammals called **primates** found food and protection from predators **up in the trees.** To help them jump from tree to tree, they developed excellent eyes—and hands that could grab. They evolved **the first thumbs.**

15 To control their wonderful eyes and hands, primates needed **larger brains.** They became more intelligent.

Perissodactyls
(PURR-iss-uh-DAK-tills):
Ungulates that have **an odd number** of toes. Horses, rhinos and tapirs are the perissodactyls living today.

Artiodactyls
(ART-ee-uh-DAK-tills):
Ungulates that have **an even number of** toes. Most ungulates living today belong to this group, which is famous for its **antlers and horns.**

Ruminants
(ROO-muh-nints):
Artiodactyls that have special teeth and **four stomachs** to help them digest grass. The world's best grass eaters!

Index